DEC 3 0 2016

D0516136

AUSTRALIAN RARE AND ENDANGERED WILDLIFE

DISCARD

GLACIER COUNTY LIBRARY
21-1ST AVE. S.E.
CUT BANK, MT. 59427

j
591.68
Par
22581

Mason Crest Publishers
www.masoncrest.com
Philadelphia

Mason Crest Publishers
370 Reed Road
Broomall, PA 19008
(866) MCP-BOOK (toll free)

Copyright © 2003 by Mason Crest Publishers.

All rights reserved. No part of this publication may be reproduced or transmitted in any form or by any means, electronic or mechanical, including photocopying, recording, taping, or any information storage and retrieval system, without permission in writing from the publisher.

First printing

ISBN 1-59084-212-X

Library of Congress Cataloging-in-Publication Data on file at the Library of Congress

First published by Steve Parish Publishing Pty Ltd
PO Box 1058, Archerfield BC
Queensland 4108, Australia
© Copyright Steve Parish Publishing Pty Ltd

Photography: Steve Parish

Photographic Assistance: Darran Leal

Front Cover: Numbat (photo Steve Parish)

Title Page: Southern Hairy-Nosed Wombat (photo Steve Parish); p. 6: M & I Morcombe; pp. 14-15: Andrew Dennis; pp. 19, 39 Hans & Judy Beste; pp. 28-29: Jiri Lochman; pp. 34-35, 35: Stan Breeden; p. 36: Raoul Slater; p. 37: Darran Leal; p. 38: Dave Watts; p. 40 (bottom right), 41: Graeme Chapman; p. 40 (bottom left): Ian Morris

Printed in Jordan

Writing, editing, design, and production by Steve Parish Publishing Pty Ltd, Australia

CONTENTS

What are rare and endangered animals?   5

Quolls   6

Bandicoots   9

Numbats   10

Wombats   13

Possums   14

Potoroos   16

Wallabies   19

Rats and mice   22

Ghost bats   25

Marine mammals   26

Western swamp turtle   28

Marine turtles   30

The malleefowl   32

Southern cassowary   35

Cockatoos   36

Parrots   39

Rare songbirds   41

Frogs   43

Could the platypus become endangered?   45

Islands are arks   46

Why are these animals vanishing?   48

What can we do to help?   49

Index of animals pictured   50

Further reading and internet resources   51

Use of Capital Letters for Animal Names in this book
An animal's official common name begins with a capital letter.
Otherwise the name begins with a lowercase letter.

WHAT ARE RARE AND ENDANGERED ANIMALS?

A rare animal is an animal that is not often seen. Perhaps there never were very many of them. Perhaps there are very few of them left in the wild. They may be spread out over a large area.

Some rare animals are in danger of disappearing altogether. These animals are said to be endangered.

Once an animal has not been seen for 50 or more years, it is said to be extinct. When this happens, it probably has vanished forever.

Endangered animals could easily become extinct. They will vanish if the place they live in is harmed or if their food disappears or if a new enemy or a disease appears.

Brush-Tailed and Burrowing Bettongs are endangered.

Both bettongs were once common on mainland Australia. Then, the bush they lived in was cleared. Dingoes, dogs, and foxes hunted them. They became rare, and today they survive in only a few places where they are safe from their enemies.

◀ A Brush-Tailed Bettong is also called a Woylie.

A Burrowing Bettong ▲

QUOLLS

Quolls are cat-sized, spotted animals that live in forests. They hunt smaller animals for food.

Most sorts of quolls are rare. The Western Quoll is endangered. There are only a few Eastern Quolls left on mainland Australia.

Quolls lose their homes when forests are cut down. They are killed by foxes and humans. Some are run over by cars at night.

Young quolls that have been bred in captivity are being put back into the wild.

The Eastern Quoll is still found in Tasmania. ▶

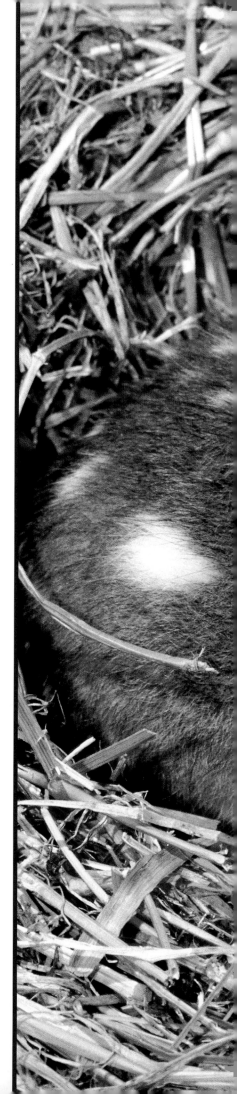

▲ The Western Quoll now lives only in forests in southwest Western Australia. This quoll has just caught a bird.

BANDICOOTS

▲ The Eastern Barred Bandicoot is rare on mainland Australia.

Because bandicoots live on the ground, they are easy prey for foxes and dogs. When the bush is cleared, so are their hiding places.

In the past 200 years, three sorts of bandicoots have become extinct. Five more sorts of bandicoots are rare or endangered.

One of the rarest bandicoots, the Bilby, lives in the desert in the center of Australia. It spends the hot day in a burrow that it has dug into the ground. At night, it comes out to find seeds and insects to eat.

◄ Cattle and rabbits destroyed much of the Bilby's habitat, and its food became scarce. It is now being bred in captivity.

NUMBATS

Most Australian animals sleep during the day and feed at night. However, Numbats sleep at night in hollow logs. They move around and feed on termites during daylight.

Numbats are found in a small area of forest in Western Australia. People are trying to save them by getting rid of the foxes in this forest that kill and eat numbats.

They are also trying to stop bushfires from burning the hollow logs in which Numbats hide and sleep.

◄ A Numbat peeping out of its shelter.

A Numbat hunting for termites. It scratches open their runways and licks them up. ▲

WOMBATS

Hairy-Nosed Wombats have short brown hairs growing on their noses.

The rare Southern Hairy-Nosed Wombat lives on the Nullarbor Plain.

The Northern Hairy-Nosed Wombat is one of Australia's most endangered animals. There are fewer than 100 living in just one small area in Queensland.

Both these wombats can only raise young ones after three years of good rain. Only then is there plenty of grass for young wombats to eat. However, cattle and sheep also eat this grass.

The place where the Northern Hairy-Nosed Wombats live has a fence around it. This keeps out the cattle and sheep, and the wombats can find grass.

▲ A Northern Hairy-Nosed Wombat

◄ A Southern Hairy-Nosed Wombat

▲ A Southern Hairy-Nosed Wombat

POSSUMS

Leadbeater's Possum ▶

Some sorts of possums can live only where they find special food and shelter.

There are only about 4,000 Leadbeater's Possums left in the wild. They need old hollow trees to nest in. However, these trees are being cut down for woodchips and timber.

There are even fewer Mountain Pygmy-Possums left—about 2,300. They should survive if their home in Australia's Alps can be kept free of fierce bushfires, weeds, and foxes.

The Lemuroid Ringtail Possum and other rainforest possums will survive as long as their rainforest homes are protected.

The Lemuroid Ringtail Possum lives only in tropical rainforests. ▶

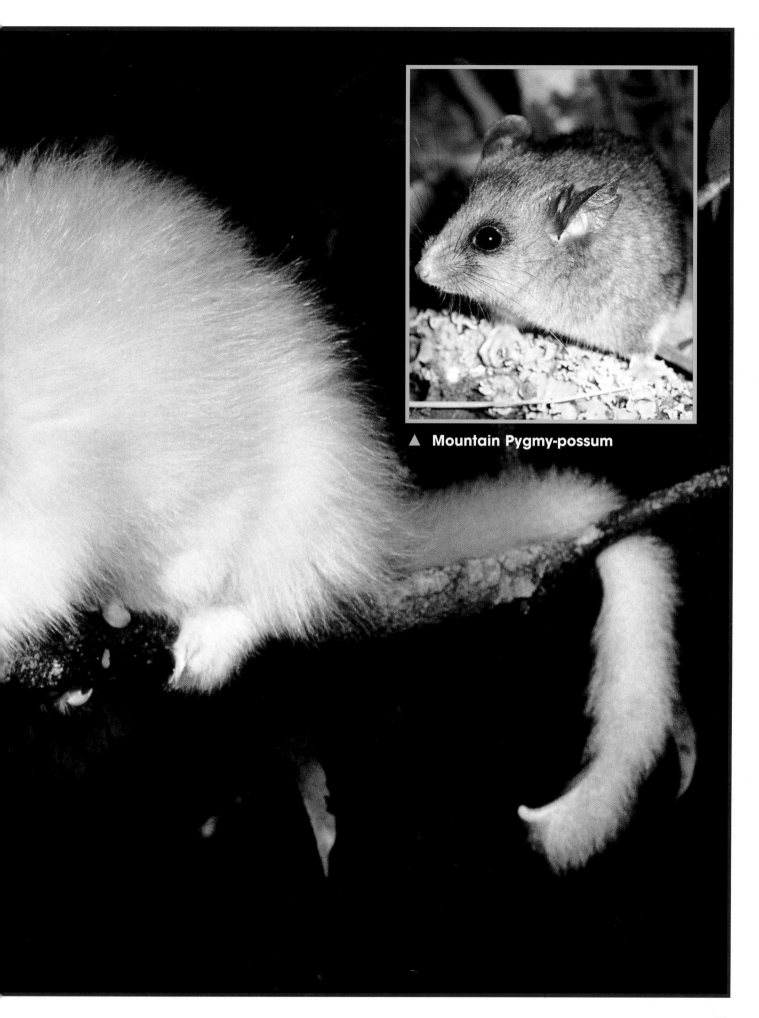

▲ **Mountain Pygmy-possum**

POTOROOS

▲ A female Long-Nosed Potoroo with a baby just out of the pouch.

Potoroos are small hopping animals that live in forests and coastal scrub. When they feed, potoroos stay close to bushes and other shelter. However, they are hunted and eaten by foxes, dingoes and dogs.

Potoroos eat the fruit of an underground fungus. This fungus helps trees and shrubs get extra food from poor soil. Potoroo droppings spread the fungus, helping the forest grow. Potoroos also eat roots and insects.

A Long-Nosed Potoroo ▶

WALLABIES

In past times, groups of Aboriginal people burned their country each year. This helped new grass grow. They hunted some wallabies, but many were left. Today, cattle, sheep, and rabbits eat the wallabies' grass.

This is only one of the reasons why some small wallabies are very rare. Some are found only in small areas in the desert or on hilly country. Others have survived only on a few islands close to the coast.

◀ The Rufous Hare-Wallaby is found on two small islands off the coast of Western Australia. People are breeding them in captivity, then putting them back in the wild in Central Australia.

▲ The Yellow-Footed Rock-Wallaby has lost much of its food to wild goats.

A Bridled Nailtail Wallaby resting in the spinifex

Bridled Nailtail Wallaby ▶

The Bridled Nailtail Wallaby rests during the day in a hollow it makes under spinifex. When it is startled, it tries to hide rather than hopping away. It was easy prey for hunters.

Today there are only about 1500 of these wallabies. They are found in just one place in central Queensland.

RATS AND MiCE

There are many native rats and mice. They do not carry disease. Only a few come near human homes. Cats and foxes prey on these small animals. Introduced mice and rats eat their food. The Greater Stick-Nest Rat is extinct on the mainland. About 1,500 survive in the wild.

▲ A Spinifex Hopping-Mouse

▲ A Plains Mouse with young ones.

A Greater Stick-Nest Rat ▶

22

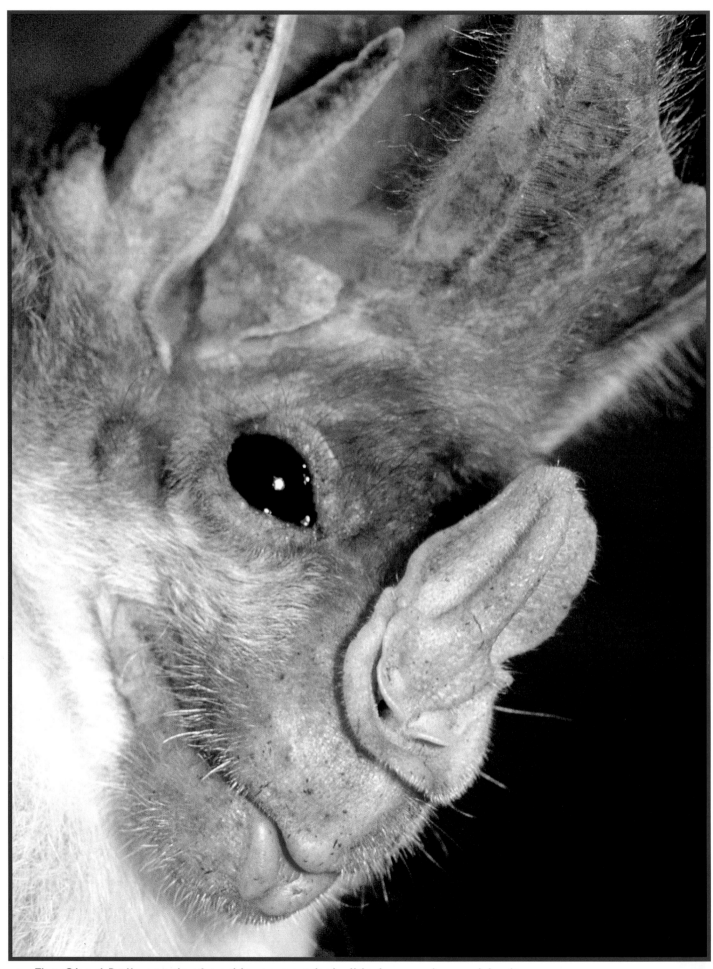

▲ The Ghost Bat's noseleaf and large ears help it to know where objects are.

GHOST BATS

◀ Ghost Bats hang upside down in caves during the day.

Ghost Bats eat insects, frogs, lizards, birds, and other bats. At night, they find prey by sending out bursts of sound. When an echo comes back from a prey animal, they can tell where it is.

During the day, Ghost Bats rest in caves and mines. When people find their home or disturb it, they leave. Once they were found in many places. Today, they are rare and endangered.

MARiNE MAMMALS

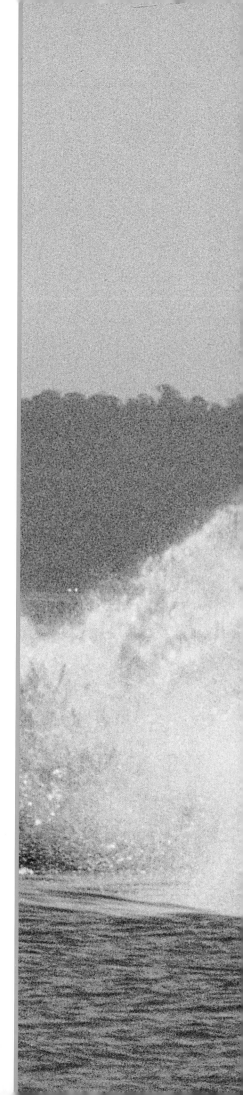

Whales have thick fat under their skins. In the past, they were hunted for the oil made from this fat. Sea lions were hunted for their fur.

Today, these marine mammals are protected. Their numbers are slowly increasing. People make special trips to see whales in the sea and sea lions on beaches.

A Humpback Whale breaching. ▶

▲ Today, there are between 3,000 and 5,000 Australian Sea Lions.

WESTERN SWAMP TURTLE

The Western Swamp Turtle is Australia's most endangered reptile. There are only about 30 turtles left in one swamp at Ellen Brook Nature Reserve, near Perth.

The swamp has been fenced against foxes and water is kept in it. It takes 10–15 years before a Western Swamp Turtle hatched in a zoo can be released in the wild.

▼ A Western Swamp Turtle

MARINE TURTLES

Six different sorts of marine turtles come to Australia's coast to lay their eggs. Five of them are endangered.

Marine turtles are drowned in fishing nets. They swallow plastic bags and oil spilled by ships.

People build houses on turtles' nesting beaches. Sometimes, turtles are killed and their eggs taken for human food.

Australia and many other countries are working to protect marine turtles.

Marine turtles, such as this Green Turtle, spend most of their lives in the sea. ▶
Only the females come on to land to lay their eggs.

▲ A Green Turtle hatchling makes for the sea. It will have to survive for many years before breeding.

THE MALLEEFOWL

The Malleefowl lives in dry, sandy country. A lot of this country has been cleared for wheat and sheep farms.

The male Malleefowl builds a huge mound of sand. In it, he makes a nest of leaves. The female lays her eggs in this nest. Each day, the male tests the heat of the nest with his tongue. If the nest is too warm, he scratches sand away. If the nest is too cool, he piles sand onto it. When the chicks hatch, they dig up out of the mound. Then they look after themselves.

Malleefowl have heavy bodies. They would rather walk than fly. In the past, humans shot them for food. Today, Malleefowl are protected by law. Foxes still hunt them. Cats kill their chicks, and monitor lizards dig up their eggs and eat them.

A Malleefowl digging into its nest mound. ▶

SOUTHERN CASSOWARY

Cassowaries are big birds that cannot fly. They live in the rainforest in tropical Queensland. Each cassowary needs a very large patch of rainforest to live in. It has to find enough fallen fruit to eat.

After a female cassowary lays eggs, the male sits on them until they hatch. Then he takes care of the chicks. He guards them and finds rainforest fruit for them to eat.

◀ ▲ The male Southern Cassowary looks after the chicks.

COCKATOOS

Cockatoos are big parrots. On their heads, they have crests of feathers. They raise their crests when they are excited.

The main food of the Glossy Black Cockatoo is the seeds of she-oak trees. If too many trees are cut down, the cockatoos will not be able to find food.

The Palm Cockatoo lives on Cape York. It is Australia's largest cockatoo. Catching and selling wild birds is against the law. However, there are still people who catch cockatoos. They smuggle them out of Australia. Then, they sell them to people who put them in cages.

▲ Palm Cockatoos eating fallen palm fruits.

A pair of Glossy Black Cockatoos. ▶

PARROTS

Today, there are only a few hundred Orange-Bellied Parrots left. They spend winter on beaches on the coast of Victoria. In summer, they fly across Bass Strait to nest in Tasmania. Their coastal habitat must be protected if they are to survive.

The Golden-Shouldered Parrot is found in parts of Cape York Peninsula. It nests in holes in termite mounds. Cattle have changed this parrot's habitat. It has also been trapped and sold as a cage bird. This is against the law.

◄ The Orange-Bellied Parrot is one of the rarest Australian birds.

▲ A pair of Golden-Shouldered Parrots on a termite mound.

▲ The rare Helmeted Honeyeater takes its name from the golden feathers on its head.

▲ Gouldian Finches eat seeds and insects.

A Western Whipbird singing. ▲

RARE SONGBIRDS

The four birds on these two pages are all endangered.

The Helmeted Honeyeater is found only along one small creek near Melbourne. There may be less than 150 left, and it is being bred in captivity.

The Gouldian Finch lives in Northern Australia. Its habitat has been altered by fire and cattle.

In the past, bird trappers caught many Gouldian Finches to sell as cagebirds.

The Noisy Scrub-Bird and the Western Whipbird both live in one small area on the coast of south-western Western Australia. Plans for a town to be built there were cancelled when the Noisy Scrub-Bird was found.

▲ A Noisy Scrub-Bird at its nest.

FROGS

At least 15 different sorts of Australian frogs are endangered. Some have not been seen at all for about 20 years. Many people believe they are extinct.

No one knows why these frogs have disappeared. There are many possible reasons.

Many of our creeks are becoming salty or dirty. Swamps are being drained. The frog-eating Cane Toad is spreading. Perhaps the sun's rays are becoming more dangerous.

There are people are working to save these endangered frogs.

◀ The Southern Day Frog was last seen in January 1979.

▲ The Northern Gastric-Brooding Frog has not been seen since 1985.

COULD THE PLATYPUS BECOME ENDANGERED?

The Platypus can still be seen in Eastern Australia's creeks and rivers. However, it has gone from many places where it once lived.

Could this famous Australian animal become endangered?

The Platypus dives in creeks and rivers to find its food. If the water becomes polluted with weed killer or fertilizer, the small animals it eats will die. So the Platypus needs clean water to catch its food in.

It also needs quiet riverbanks in which to dig its burrow. The female lays her eggs in a nest in a special part of the burrow.

Like many other animals, the Platypus needs to be looked after. Its habitat needs to be protected. If creeks and rivers are kept clean, then the Platypus will go on living there.

◀ When a Platypus walks or digs, it folds its foot-webs back to protect them.

When a Platypus swims, ▲ its feet unfold into paddles.

45

ISLANDS ARE ARKS

▲ The outcrops of rock where rock wallabies, such as this Black-Footed, live are often separated by plains, desert, and farms.

Islands are pieces of land cut off by water from the mainland. Animals that live on islands are protected from many enemies.

Tasmania is Australia's biggest island. The Tasmanian Devil still survives there. It once lived on mainland Australia, but when the dingo arrived, the Devil died out.

Rainforests are like islands of trees. They provide special food for animals that cannot survive in any other sort of habitat.

Australia has many rocky hills that stand like islands above "seas" of desert or farmland. They are home to rock wallabies and other rare animals.

Sometimes, forest is cut down or burned. Sometimes, there is no food or water left in rocky hills. Without their "island" homes, the animals may not survive.

▲ The Green Ringtail Possum can survive only in tropical rainforest.

▲ The Tasmanian Devil disappeared from the mainland after the dingo arrived.

47

WHY ARE THESE ANIMALS VANISHING?

▲ Once their homes are gone, most animals cannot live in a place any more.

▲ Cats and foxes kill wildlife. Other harmful feral animals are goats, pigs, and rabbits.

When a wild animal loses the wild place it lives in, it usually has nowhere to go. Even if it finds another place with the food and shelter it needs, there will be other animals there already.

There are fewer and fewer wild places for wild creatures. One reason is that there are more and more people.

Humans are taking over the wild places. They make clean places dirty with their waste. They poison water with chemicals and salt. They cut down the trees and clear the land.

Feral animals, such as foxes and cats, kill wildlife. Rabbits and farm animals eat the plants wild animals depend on for food.

48

WHAT CAN WE DO TO HELP?

▲ A family learning about wildlife habitat.

All of us can help save Australia's endangered wildlife.

One of the easiest things to do is to make sure the cat is kept inside the house at night. Put a bell on its neck to warn any animals it tries to hunt.

Don't let your dog run wild in the bush. Even small dogs will chase and kill wild animals.

Learn all you can about Australian wildlife as well as wildlife in your own area. You can keep a wild area in your garden and watch the animals that come to live there. Visit places where people who care are saving endangered wildlife.

Knowing about endangered animals is the first step in helping to save them.

INDEX OF ANIMALS PICTURED

Bandicoot, Eastern Barred 9
Bat, Ghost 24, 25
Bettong, Brush-Tailed 4
    Burrowing 5
Bilby 8–9
Black Cockatoo, Glossy 37
Cassowary, Southern 34–35, 35
Cat, feral 48
Cockatoo, Palm 36
Devil, Tasmanian 49
Finch, Gouldian 40
Frog, Northern Gastric-Brooding 43
    Southern Day 42
Hare-Wallaby, Rufous 18
Honeyeater, Helmeted 40
Hopping-Mouse, Spinifex 22
Malleefowl 32–33
Mouse, Plains 22
Numbat 10, 10–11
Parrot, Golden-Shouldered 39
    Orange-Bellied 38
Platypus 44, 45
Possum, Green Ringtail 47
    Leadbeater's 14
    Lemuroid Ringtail 14–15
Potoroo, Long-Nosed 16, 17
Pygmy-Possum, Mountain 15
Quoll, Eastern 6–7
    Western 6
Rat, Greater Stick-Nest 23

Rock Wallaby, Black-Footed 46
    Yellow-Footed 19
Scrub-Bird, Noisy 41
Sea Lion, Australian 26
Turtle, Green 30, 31
    Western Swamp 28–29
Wallaby, Bridled Nailtail 20, 20–21
Whale, Humpback 26–27
Whipbird, Western 40
Wombat, Northern Hairy-Nosed 13
    Southern Hairy-Nosed 3, 12, 13

FURTHER READING & INTERNET RESOURCES

For more information on Australia's animals, check out the following books and Web sites.

Spillman, David and Mark Wilson (illustrator). *Yellow-Eye.* (September 2001) Crocodile Books (Inteu); ISBN: 1566564107

When the numbers of the Yellow-Eye Fish begin to decline, white men and aborigines must work together to come up with a solution.

Arnold, Caroline. *Australian Animals.* (August 2000) HarperCollins Juvenile Books; ISBN: 0688167667

Seventeen unusual animals from Australia are introduced in this full-color book, including koalas, possums, gliders, quolls, Tasmanian devils, platypuses, echidnas, kangaroos, wombats, dingoes, snakes, and penguins.

Morpurgo, Michael, Christian Birmingham (illustrator). *Wombat Goes Walkabout.* (April 2000) Candlewick Press; ISBN: 0763611689

As Wombat wanders through the Australian bush in search of his mother, he encounters a variety of creatures demanding to know who he is and what he can do.

Langeland, Deidre, Frank Ordaz (illustrator), and Ranye Kaye (narrator). *Kangaroo Island: The Story of an Australian Mallee Forest.* (April 1998) Soundprints Corp. Audio; ISBN: 156899544X

As morning comes to Kangaroo Island following a thunderstorm, a mother kangaroo finds her lost baby, and a burned eucalyptus tree sprouts buds and becomes a new home for animals. The cassette that comes with the book adds sounds of sea lions barking, sea gulls calling, crickets humming, and even a raging forest fire.

http://www.zip.com.au/~elanora/ewild.html

This site contains pictures and articles drawn and researched by students at Elanora Heights Primary School. It is perfect for younger viewers and contains tidbits of information on all sorts of endangered animals living in Australia.

http://www.esl.com.au/savewildlife.htm

Earth Sanctuaries are a private alternative to the national parks system in Australia. A special vermin-proof fence is built around the perimeter of each sanctuary to keep out foxes, cats, and rabbits. To find links to more information on specific rare and endangered Australian animals, scroll down to Saving Wildlife.

http://www.billabongsanctuary.com.au/cassowary.asp

The Southern Cassowary is one of Australia's most endangered species. This page on the Billabong Sanctuary Web site provides some background information on this large bird, reasons why it has become endangered, and what this Australian facility is doing to counteract this.

http://www.viridans.com.au/RAREAN/Varare01.htm

This site features information on rare and endangered species in Victoria. It provides an overview as to what makes a species considered extinct, endangered, or rare, and, by clicking the pictures next to each line of text, viewers can read more in-depth information on an animal.

http://www.australianaustralia.com/fauna.html#endangspecies

This fascinating article—one page in an entire site dedicated to all things Australian—discusses what efforts have been undertaken to restore several of Australia's endangered species, including Burrowing Bettongs, Western Barred Bandicoots, the Greater Stick Nest Rat, the Richmond Birdwing Butterfly, and the Grey-Headed Flying Fox.

NATURE KIDS SERIES

Birdlife

Australia is home to some of the most interesting, colorful, and noisy birds on earth. Discover some of the many different types, including parrots, kingfishers, and owls.

Frogs and Reptiles

Australia has a wide variety of environments, and there is at least one frog or reptile that calls each environment home. Discover the frogs and reptiles living in Australia.

Kangaroos and Wallabies

The kangaroo is one of the most well-known Australian creatures. Learn interesting facts about kangaroos and wallabies, a close cousin.

Marine Fish

The ocean surrounding Australia is home to all sorts of marine fish. Discover their interesting shapes, sizes, and colors, and learn about the different types of habitat in the ocean.

Rainforest Animals

Australia's rainforests are home to a wide range of animals, including snakes, birds, frogs, and wallabies. Discover a few of the creatures that call the rainforests home.

Rare & Endangered Wildlife

Animals all over the world need our help to keep from becoming extinct. Learn about the special creatures in Australia that are in danger of disappearing forever.

Sealife

Australia is surrounded by sea. As a result, there is an amazing variety of life that lives in these waters. Dolphins, crabs, reef fish, and eels are just a few of the animals highlighted in this book.

Wildlife

Australia is known for its unique creatures, such as the kangaroo and the koala. Read about these and other special creatures that call Australia home.